AISHA AND THE ANCESTORS

A BIRTHDAY PARTY FOR GREAT GANNY!

Written by
Nicole Y. Walters

Illustrated by
Steven Luna

Published by
Bright Fame, LLC.

Text copyright © 2021 by Nicole Y. Walters
Illustrations copyright © 2021 by Steven Luna
All rights reserved.

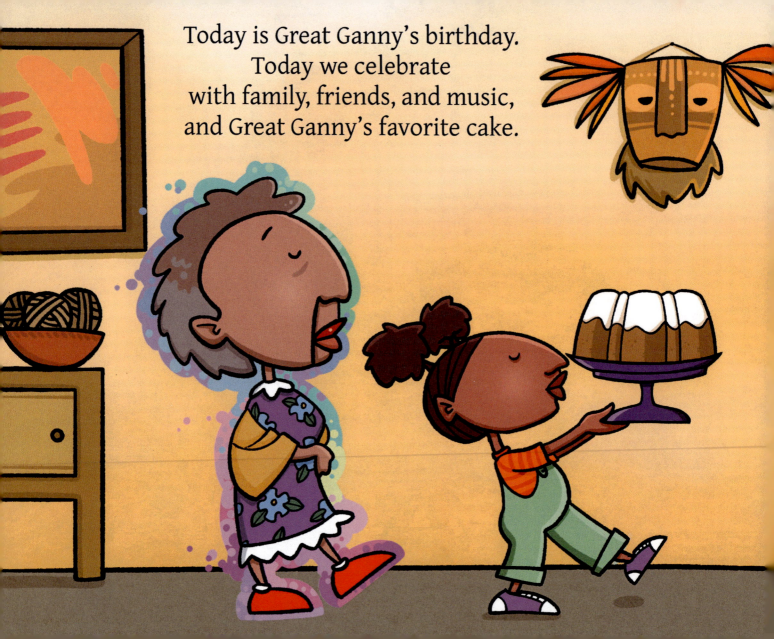

Today is Great Ganny's birthday.
Today we celebrate
with family, friends, and music,
and Great Ganny's favorite cake.

Daddy fried Great Ganny's famous chicken. Great Gandy boiled her greens.

Uncle Ronnie dances with his cane as we clap and sing along.

Go, Uncle Ronnie!

...even though now she is gone.

My grandma lights a white candle.
My Great Gandy says a prayer.

Aunt Tasha tells us stories about Great Ganny when she was still here.

My Great Ganny was AMAZING!

Today is Great Ganny's birthday, and though we celebrate Dad says that it's okay to cry and be sad that she's away.

Our ancestors love and guide us.
They help us to succeed.
And every time we remember them,
we bless their memory.

Dad says I look like Great Ganny. "It's the sparkle in your eye.

When you smile,
I see her smile,
and I know that she's nearby."

Happy birthday, Great Ganny!

Buttermilk Fried Chicken
Chef Devin Smith

Be sure to only cook with help from Mom and Dad when you try Great Ganny's delicious recipe!

Ingredients

- 3lbs chicken pieces (I prefer dark meat)
- 1 cup hot sauce
- 2 cups buttermilk
- 3 cups all-purpose flour
- 2 teaspoons smoked paprika
- 2 teaspoons onion powder
- 2 teaspoons garlic powder
- Italian seasoning, to taste
- Tony Chachere's MORE SPICE Creole Seasoning
- 4 cups canola oil or peanut oil

Directions

1. Rinse chicken pieces and pat dry with paper towels.
2. Place chicken in a plastic snap or zip bag (no more than 4 in a bag); add hot sauce and buttermilk, mix, seal and place in refrigerator for two hours or overnight.
3. Combine the flour, smoked paprika, garlic powder, onion powder, Italian seasoning, and Creole seasoning in a bowl and mix with a fork until blended.
4. After chicken is done marinating, pour all contents into another bowl.
5. Add oil to a cast iron or heavy bottomed skillet and heat on medium high until oil is at 350 degrees.
6. In batches, coat chicken in seasoned flour, shake off excess, and place in skillet; fry for 8-10 minutes on each side, or when cooked through.
7. Once cooked through, place on cooling rack until ready to serve.

Questions and Conversations

A Birthday Party For Great Ganny! features multi-generational, family relationships with siblings, parents, grandparents, etc. How much do you know about your family? Have you ever created a family tree?

The Brown family has gathered to remember Great Ganny on her birthday even though she has passed away. Does your family have any traditions to remember loved ones who have transitioned?

Matthew comforts Aisha by reminding her that she and her departed Great Ganny have a lot in common. Have you ever talked with your child about what he/she/they have in common with members of your ancestry?

Did any of your favorite ancestors have a special recipe? Can you make it together with your family? Can you create a recipe yourself?

There are many ways to honor our ancestors. In A Birthday Party For Great Ganny!, the Brown family use their altar, food, and music to remember Great Ganny. What are some other ways we can venerate our ancestors?

Thank you to my ancestors, known and unknown. I stand upon your shoulders. I live through your strength. I am because of your love.

To my father, Robert Andrew Conard, may the light which guided you in life ever precede you.

Special acknowledgements to Elemi Gayle of Yeyeo Botanica for spiritual consultation and to Chef Devin Smith of Creole for the Soul for his recipe contribution.

Aisha and the Ancestors is delighted to feature prominent African American ancestors who made positive contributions to all of American culture. Please visit www.aishaandtheancestors.com/ourcommonancestors to learn about the ancestors acknowledged in A Birthday Party For Great Ganny!

About the Creators

Nicole Y. Walters

Nicole Y. Walters understood the world was a magical place from an early age. The descendent of a long line of preachers, she grew up in the church where words like spirit, ghost, saints, angels, miracles, and prayer were as commonplace as hello and good morning. As a child, Nicole was fascinated with mythology of all kinds and lived in the hopeful expectation of encounters with the Divine.

Today, Nicole brings her sense of wonder and curiosity to everything she does. When she's not writing books, writing songs, or singing jazz, Nicole loves to spend time with her grandchildren who are, themselves, quite magical.

Steven Luna

Steven Luna is the kid who never stopped drawing. In fact, he's probably drawing something right this very minute! He believes in everything, which makes the world a wonderful place to behold. He hopes his drawings add to the wonder of the world, too! More than anything, he believes in Aisha's journey and all the incredible lessons the Brown family can teach about family, ancestor veneration, celebration, and love.

For fun activities, information about the creators, and learning opportunities related to ancestor veneration, please check out www.aishaandtheancestors.com and follow along on social media!

Facebook:
www.facebook.com/aishaandtheancestors

Instagram
@authornicoleywalters
@stevenlunaillustration

Tik Tok:
@nicoleconardwalters